The Little One's
BIBLE

with "talkabouts"
and prayers

Eira Reeves

PROMISE
PRESS

CONTENTS

OLD TESTAMENT

NEW TESTAMENT

In the very beginning

In the very beginning there was only darkness.

Do you like it when it is night-time? How does it make you feel?

DEAR GOD, please be with me when it's dark. Amen.

Then God made light. It was very good.
Now there was night and day.

What do you enjoy doing in the daytime?

PLEASE GOD, help me to be good in the day and sleep
at night. Amen.

On day two, God made the sky.
It was a beautiful color.

Have you looked at the sky today?
Can you describe the color?

THANK YOU, GOD, for the big and
wonderful sky. Amen.

Then on day three, God made the land,
the sea, and the clouds in the air.

Do you like the sea best when it is calm or stormy?

DEAR GOD, thank You for the land, sea,
and clouds. Amen.

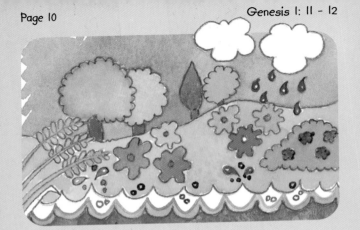

Also on day three, God made the
grass, flowers, and trees.

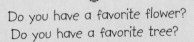

Do you have a favorite flower?
Do you have a favorite tree?

THANK YOU, GOD, for all the different
colors and shapes. Amen.

On the fourth day, God created the sun and the moon.

What do you like about the sun? What do you like about the moon?

THANK YOU, GOD, that we know when it's morning and evening. Amen.

On the fifth day, God made all the fish that swim in the sea.

Look at the big fish at the top.
Do you know its name?

DEAR GOD, thank You for all the beautiful fish
that You have made. Amen.

Then on the same day, God made lots
of birds that fly in the sky.

Do you know what kind of bird is sitting on
the branch?

THANK YOU, GOD, for my favorite bird
called . . . Amen.

When it was the sixth day,
God made all the
animals . . . so many kinds!

What is your favorite animal and why?

THANK YOU, GOD, for the smallest animal and
the largest. Amen.

On the same day, God created a man
and a woman, called Adam and Eve.

God wanted to bless them both. How does
God bless you?

YOU ARE SUCH a big and clever God to make
such a wonderful earth. Amen.

Then on the seventh day, God
took a rest. He was very pleased
with His work.

When you take a rest, what do you like to do?

THANK YOU, GOD, that You like us to take a day of
rest just like You did. Amen.

Isn't God great? He made a big garden for Adam and Eve to enjoy.

Do you like gardens? How many games can
you play in a garden?

THANK YOU, GOD, for making such a beautiful garden
for Adam and Eve. Amen.

One day Adam and Eve were naughty. They disobeyed God.

Have you seen somebody being naughty today?
What did they do?

DEAR GOD, help me to be good every day so that I can make You happy. Amen.

God was very sad with Adam and Eve.
His garden had been spoilt by them.

What makes you sad? Can you tell
someone about it?

THANK YOU, GOD, that You always want to
help me when I am sad. Amen.

Trouble had come into the world. Adam and Eve had to leave God's garden.

What are some of the bad things in this world?

THANK YOU, GOD, that I know whatever happens, You will take care of me. Amen.

Noah and his BIG, BIG boat

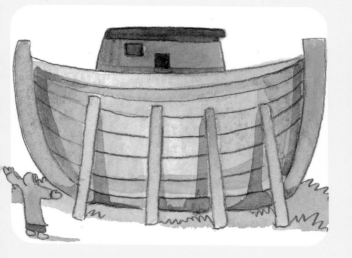

This is Noah. He was a good man and he loved God very much.

How do you let God know that you love Him?

DEAR GOD, every day I just want to say that I love You. Amen.

Noah lived amongst some bad people.
God was very upset with them.

Another time that God was sad with some
people was . . . Look at page 19.

I AM SO SORRY, GOD, that when people do bad things,
You get sad. Amen.

God told Noah that He was going to get rid of all these bad people.

But God was going to save Noah. Why? . . .
Look at page 22.

THANK YOU, GOD, that You planned to protect Noah. Amen.

God also told Noah to build a boat. He and his family would be safe in it.

Have you ever been in a boat? What did you enjoy about it?

THANK YOU, GOD, for helping Noah and giving him the plans for the boat. Amen.

So Noah built a boat. His family helped him. It was a BIG, BIG boat.

God was pleased with Noah. Do you know why? Read the verse above.

DEAR GOD, help me to listen to You, just like Noah did. Amen.

Then God told Noah to take his family, and two of every animal and bird on to the boat.

Can you imagine what the people in Noah's village thought?

THANK YOU, GOD, that Noah kept on obeying You. Amen.

When Noah, his family, and all of
the animals were on the boat . . .
it began to rain.

What do you enjoy about the rain?
What don't you enjoy about it?

THANK YOU, GOD, for keeping Noah dry
when it rained. Amen.

It rained and it rained and it rained . . .
And the whole earth was flooded.

What happens when there is a flood? Have you
heard of one recently?

DEAR FATHER GOD, thank You for keeping
Noah and his family safe. Amen.

It rained for forty days and forty nights. Everything on the earth was flooded.

What do you think is happening on the boat?

THANK YOU, GOD, for looking after every animal and bird on Noah's BIG, BIG boat. Amen.

Finally it stopped raining, and Noah's boat landed on top of a mountain.

Are you happy when it stops raining?
Why are you happy?

DEAR GOD, You are so powerful because You make it rain and You stop it. Amen.

Genesis 8: 8 - 9

After a while, Noah wanted to
know if the water had gone down.
So he sent out a dove.

How do you think Noah felt when it stopped raining?

THANK YOU, GOD, that Noah trusted You. Help me to
trust You like Noah. Amen.

Finally, the dove returned with
a leaf . . . so Noah knew the earth
was getting dry.

What do you think was Noah's next plan?

DEAR GOD, thank You that You didn't forget Noah, his
family, and all the animals and birds. Amen.

Hooray! Noah let all the animals and
birds on to the dry ground.

God made a new day for Noah. What do you
like about a new day?

THANK YOU, DEAR GOD, for each new
day with You. Amen.

Noah thanked God for keeping them
all safe during the flood.

Would you like to thank God for something today?

DEAR GOD, it's so good that I can come to You and
thank You for. . .Amen.

God then made a rainbow.
He promised never again to flood
all of the earth.

Have you ever made a promise? Did you keep it?

THANK YOU, GOD, for always keeping Your
promises to me. Amen.

Abraham, who followed God

Meet Abram who was married to
Sarai. They lived in a place called Ur.

Do you live in a village, town, or city? Why do
you like living there?

DEAR GOD, thank You for my village/town/city. Amen.

Abram and Sarai were very sad
because they didn't have any children.

Perhaps you could become a special friend to someone.

PLEASE, GOD, let us know that we belong to
your family. Amen.

One day, God told Abram to pack up
and go to a new country.

Do you enjoy packing your bags when you go away?

THANK YOU, GOD, for always being with us
wherever we go. Amen.

Abram trusted God, so he left with his family, servants, and animals.

What do you like about a new adventure?

THANK YOU, GOD, that You spoke to Abram and he obeyed You. Amen.

On arriving in the new country, there was a quarrel on how to divide the land.

Have you ever had a quarrel? How did you feel?

THANK YOU, GOD, that You see right inside our hearts. Amen.

So Abram gave Lot, his nephew,
the first choice of the land.
Lot chose the best.

Do you always let friends have the first choice?

THANK YOU, GOD, that Abram didn't take the best bit of
land for himself. Amen.

God spoke to Abram again.
He told Abram that one day he
would have a son.

What good news do you like to hear? Why does it
make you happy?

THANK YOU, GOD, for bringing good news and
promises. Amen.

Abram believed God, even though he
was very, very, very old!

How old do you think the people are who
take care of you?

THANK YOU, GOD, whatever our age, we are always
important to You. Amen.

God told Abram that his family would be more than ALL the stars in the sky!

Have you ever tried to count the stars? What number did you get to?

THANK YOU, GOD, that You encouraged Abram. Amen.

Then God changed Abram's name to Abraham. It means "father of many."

How many are there in your family? What are their names?

DEAR GOD, we are glad that each of us is very special to You. Amen.

God blessed Abraham with many
animals and gold. Abraham was
God's friend.

God would like to be your friend. Do you talk to
Him every day?

THANK YOU, GOD, that we can come to
You as a friend. Amen.

Just as God had promised,
Abraham and his wife had a baby
boy called Isaac. This was a miracle!

As they were both old how do you think
Abraham and his wife felt?

THANK YOU, GOD, for Your amazing miracles! Amen.

Isaac grew up and was a great help to his mom and dad.

How do you enjoy helping your mom and dad?

PLEASE GOD, show us how to help other people. Amen.

Later on, Isaac married Rebekah.
Abraham was very pleased and
gave a big party.

What was your favorite party and why?

THANK YOU, GOD, that You love us to celebrate. Amen.

And so through Abraham, God's special family grew and GREW and GREW!

🐝

Do you remember God's promise? Look at page 46.

THANK YOU, GOD, that You are such a giving God. Amen.

Jacob and his dream

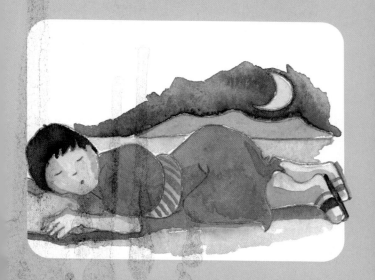

Isaac and Rebekah had two baby
boys . . . They were twins called
Esau and Jacob.

Do you know any twins? What are their names?

THANK YOU, GOD, for twins everywhere.
Please bless them. Amen.

Esau was just a little older than Jacob.
As twins, they did not look alike at all.

Have you ever seen twins? Could you tell the difference
between them?

WHOEVER WE ARE, DEAR GOD, You love us
all the same. Amen.

The twins were very different. Esau was
lively and Jacob was very quiet.

What do you enjoy doing when you are busy? What do
you enjoy doing while sitting still?

THANK YOU FOR being with us, God, when we are
busy and when we are quiet. Amen.

As they grew older, Esau and Jacob
enjoyed doing different things.

How do you do things differently from your friends?

DEAR GOD, thank You for making us
all so different. Amen.

Esau loved to go hunting, and Jacob
loved to stay at home.

When you are outside, what do you like to do? When
you are indoors what do you like to do?

DEAR GOD, whatever we do, we want to
please You. Amen.

The father wanted to bless Esau,
the eldest twin, and give him all
that he owned.

Name times when you have been blessed by
someone special.

HEAVENLY FATHER, You always want to bless us.
Thank You. Amen.

Rebekah, the mom, wasn't happy. She wanted Jacob to have the blessing.

Jacob was Rebekah's favorite twin. What is your favorite toy?

THANK YOU, GOD, that all of Your children are favorites. Amen.

So Rebekah told Jacob to play a trick
on his blind father.
He pretended to be Esau.

Has anyone ever played a trick on you?
How did you feel?

PLEASE GOD, help me always to be kind to
other people. Amen.

When Esau found out about the trick,
he was furious with his brother.

What do you think Jacob should have said to Esau?

DEAR GOD, teach us to say we are sorry when we have
done something wrong. Amen.

Rebekah told Jacob to run away quickly.
She said goodbye to her favorite son.

What do you feel like when you say
goodbye to someone?

DEAR GOD, help me not to be sad when
people go away. Amen.

Jacob ran and ran. One night he
stopped to sleep in the desert.

What do you think a desert looks like?

HEAVENLY FATHER, thank You for being with us
when we sleep. Amen.

Jacob dreamed there was a stairway
from heaven with lots of angels.

What do you think God was saying to
Jacob in the dream?

DEAR GOD, You are always there to protect us.
Thank You. Amen.

Jacob went to live with his uncle . . .
He married and had twelve sons.

Do you have an uncle? What is his name?

THANK YOU, GOD, for putting us in families. Amen.

Jacob wanted to go back home. But he thought that Esau would still be angry.

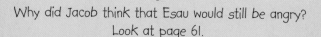

Why did Jacob think that Esau would still be angry?
Look at page 61.

THANK YOU, GOD, for encouraging me when I am worried. Amen.

Jacob did return home.
Esau gave him such a welcome.
They were then friends.

What happy times have you had with your family?

THANK YOU, GOD, that Esau had forgiven
Jacob in his heart. Amen.

Joseph and his amazing coat

Jacob loved his twelve sons, but Joseph,
the youngest, was his favorite.

How do you think the other sons felt?

THANK YOU, GOD, for loving each of us the same. Amen.

So, Jacob made a beautiful coat for Joseph. It had amazing colors.

Can you think of something that someone special has done for you?

THANK YOU, GOD, for those who look after me. Amen.

Joseph's brothers were jealous and sold
him to passing traders to be a slave.

What do you think a slave's job is?

GOD HAD a special plan for Joseph's life.
Thank You, God. Amen.

Joseph was bought by a man named Potiphar, who lived in Egypt.

Have you ever traveled to another country?
What happened?

DEAR HEAVENLY FATHER, You are always with
us when we travel. Amen.

Potiphar's wife behaved badly. She said
some untrue things about Joseph.

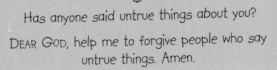

Has anyone said untrue things about you?

DEAR GOD, help me to forgive people who say
untrue things. Amen.

So Potiphar had Joseph put away in prison. He must have been very unhappy.

Do you think that God was still watching over Joseph?

DEAR GOD, I pray for every prisoner in prison. Amen.

Sometime later, Pharaoh, the king of
Egypt, had some very strange dreams.

Can you tell someone about a dream that
you have had?

WHETHER WE HAVE good or bad dreams, You are with us.
THANK YOU, GOD. Amen.

So Pharaoh called Joseph out of prison to ask him the meaning of his dreams.

Do you think Joseph was pleased to be out of prison?

THANK YOU, GOD, for trusting Joseph. Amen.

"The dreams mean," said Joseph,
"that you will have plenty of food for
seven years ..."

Do you think that Pharaoh was pleased with this?
Why?

THANK YOU, GOD, that You provide all our needs. Amen.

" . . . and you will have seven years with no food," continued Joseph.

Now how do you think Pharaoh felt?

DEAR GOD, please help us to look after people who have nothing. Amen.

Pharaoh thought Joseph was great, so he put him in charge of all the food.

Do you know of anyone who is in charge?

THANK YOU, GOD, for all those you put in charge. Amen.

One day, Joseph's brothers set off to Egypt looking for food to buy.

Do you like buying food? What is your favorite food?

DEAR GOD, thank You for all the food You give us. Amen.

When Joseph saw his brothers, he
pretended to be angry.

Do you know why Joseph was angry?
Look at page 72.

THANK YOU, GOD, that Joseph only pretended to
be angry. Amen.

At first, Joseph's brothers were
upset because they didn't see that
it was Joseph.

Have you ever been upset? Can you say why?

DEAR HEAVENLY FATHER, I know You always help us when
we are upset. Amen.

Suddenly, they knew it was their long
lost brother, Joseph.
What a happy meeting!

When was your last happy meeting with someone?

DEAR GOD, thank You for all the happy
meetings I have had. Amen.

Moses, the great leader

One day an Egyptian princess found a
Hebrew baby in the river.

The princess called the baby Moses. What is your
favorite name?

DEAR GOD, thank You for knowing each one of
us by name. Amen.

Moses grew up to be a prince. He lived
in a very grand palace in Egypt.

Do you know who lives in palaces?

HEAVENLY FATHER, thank You for kings, queens,
princes, and princesses. Amen.

Moses' people, the Hebrews, were
slaves in Egypt. Moses thought
this was unfair.

Have you ever seen anything unfair?

DEAR GOD, please help people who suffer
because of unkindness. Amen.

One day, Moses ran away from the palace and he became a shepherd.

Look at the picture. How many sheep can you count?

THANK YOU, HEAVENLY FATHER, for all Your sheep. Amen.

There was a bush on fire, and God
spoke to Moses from the flames.

God was about to make Moses a leader. Do you
know of any leaders?

THANK YOU, GOD, for people who look
after everyone. Amen.

God said to Moses, "Go to Pharaoh
and tell him to let my people go."

Who are the people God was talking about?
Look at page 88.

THANK YOU, GOD, for rescuing the
Hebrew people. Amen.

"No," said Pharaoh, "I will not let your people go." He refused several times.

Moses asked again and again. Why was this?
Look at page 91.

THANK YOU, GOD, that Moses heard You and obeyed You. Amen.

So God sent trouble to Pharaoh and his people . . . like swarms of flies and frogs!

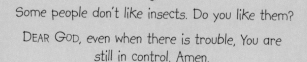

Some people don't like insects. Do you like them?

DEAR GOD, even when there is trouble, You are still in control. Amen.

... And then more trouble, like bad storms with hail and lightning!

Do you like lightning? What don't you like about it?

THANK YOU, GOD, for keeping Moses and his people safe. Amen.

Finally, Pharaoh gave up his idea and told Moses, "Go with your people."

Have you ever given up doing something? What was it that you gave up doing?

THANK YOU, HEAVENLY FATHER, that You gave courage to Moses. Amen.

At last, Moses led his people out of
Egypt. They were all so happy!

What would you have said if you were following Moses?

PLEASE GOD, let me always be thankful to
You for everything. Amen.

Then the Egyptians chased after Moses' people. But God opened up the sea and they all escaped.

God solved another problem!
What problem has God solved for you?

THANK YOU, GOD, that You take care of my problems. Amen.

On the way home to Israel, God gave Moses some rules for his people.

These rules are called the Ten Commandments. What rules does your family have?

THANK YOU, GOD, for giving us a good way to live. Amen.

One of the rules God gave was that children should respect their parents.

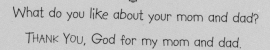

What do you like about your mom and dad?

THANK YOU, God for my mom and dad.

Moses was a great leader! God had
protected and guided His people.

In what ways does God protect you?

THANK YOU, GOD, that You watch over me and
protect me. Amen.

Ruth and Naomi

Naomi and her family lived in
Bethlehem. One day they left to look
for food in Moab.

Do you know of any countries where there
isn't much food?

DEAR GOD, please help those people who don't
have enough to eat. Amen.

The family settled in Moab, and
Naomi's sons got married to
Ruth and Orpah.

Do you know of anyone who has recently married?

PLEASE, GOD, be with all of those who
are married. Amen.

But something very sad happened.
The husbands of Naomi, Ruth, and
Orpah died.

How do you think all three of these women felt?

THANK YOU, GOD, for giving us comfort when something
sad happens. Amen.

Now Naomi wanted to return to Bethlehem and Ruth went with her.

Ruth comforted Naomi. Do you have a friend like that?

DEAR HEAVENLY FATHER, thank You for my special friend. Amen.

In Bethlehem, Ruth gathered barley from fields belonging to Boaz, a rich farmer.

Have you ever been on a farm?

THANK YOU, GOD, for all the food gathered from farms. Amen.

Boaz knew that Ruth was poor, so he
told his workers to help her.

Do you know anyone who is poor whom you can help?

PLEASE, GOD, help all the poor people in
the world. Amen.

Boaz even offered food to Ruth. She
was so grateful to him.

Name some things that you are grateful for.

DEAR GOD, thank You for feeding Ruth and me. Amen.

Ruth returned home to Naomi with lots of food. Boaz had been so kind.

Name some of the kind things that have happened to you.

THANK YOU, GOD, for all of your kindness and provision. Amen.

Naomi wanted Ruth to marry. She said that Boaz would be a good husband.

Why would Boaz be a good husband for Ruth?
Look at page 109.

PLEASE, GOD, help us to be kind to one another. Amen.

But now, Ruth was a foreigner, so
Boaz had to explain this to
the local people.

What do you think the word "foreigner" means?

PLEASE, GOD, make me welcome visitors always who
come to my country. Amen.

The people in charge of the town gave
their blessing. Boaz married Ruth.

Have you been to a wedding? What did you
like about the day?

THANK YOU, GOD, for all the people who are
getting married. Amen.

Naomi, quite an elderly lady, was so pleased that they had married.

Do you have a grandmother or grandfather?
How do you help them?

DEAR GOD, please take care of older
people everywhere. Amen.

Later, Ruth had a baby. Boaz was so proud and Naomi was delighted.

Do you know anyone who has a baby?
How old is the baby?

DEAR GOD, please take care of all the
babies in the world. Amen.

Ruth and Boaz named the baby Obed,
meaning "servant of the Lord."

If you had a baby brother or sister, what
name would you choose?

THANK YOU, GOD, that you know us
each by our name. Amen.

Naomi, Obed's grandmother, helped to look after him. She was so happy.

Do you know an elderly person? What do you enjoy doing with that person?

PLEASE, GOD, bless and care for all grandparents and make them happy. Amen.

David, the shepherd

David, the shepherd, lived in Bethlehem
with his seven brothers.

Name different things David had to do as a shepherd.

THANK YOU, GOD, for shepherds and
sheep everywhere. Amen.

To pass the time away, David played
the harp and sang songs.

David wrote Psalm 23. Let someone read it to you.
What do you like about it?

DEAR HEAVENLY FATHER, thank You for being our
Shepherd. Amen.

There was such love in David's heart for God.

Do you think that God can see right into your heart?

DEAR GOD, thank You for knowing what I
feel and think. Amen.

One day, a friend ran to David with a
very urgent message.

If you had an urgent message for a friend, what
would you say?

THANK YOU, GOD, for helping me to love You
like David. Amen.

There's a special visitor named Samuel who wants to see you," said the friend.

Do you have special visitors come to your home? What are their names?

DEAR GOD, thank You for all the special times when visitors come. Amen.

Samuel said that one day David would be king of Israel!

How do you think David felt about this news?

THANK YOU, GOD, that You can use me for special jobs too. Amen.

During some fighting, David took some food to his brothers. He was frightened.

Has there ever been a time when you have been frightened?

DEAR GOD, let me ask You for help when I am frightened. Amen.

One of the enemies was a big giant
man called Goliath.
Everyone was scared of him.

Are you scared about anything? If you tell God,
He will understand.

PLEASE, GOD, help me to be brave when
I am scared. Amen.

"I'll fight Goliath," said David. He
totally trusted in God to win the fight.

Discuss some of the times you have trusted God.

DEAR GOD, help me to trust You always as
David did. Amen.

Goliath laughed and laughed. He was
SO big and David was SO small.

Has anyone made fun of you or laughed at you? Talk to
someone about it.

DEAR GOD, please help me to be strong at times. Amen.

David was very brave. He fought
Goliath and killed him!

Why was David so brave? Look at page 126.

THANK YOU, GOD, for David's courage and
strength. Amen.

The battle was won. Everyone waved
and cheered at David's bravery.

Has there been a time when you have cheered?
Why did you cheer?

THANK YOU, GOD, that You were on David's side. Amen.

Sometime later, David became king of
Israel, just as Samuel had said.

Can you remember when Samuel told David this?
Look at page 123.

DEAR GOD, thank You for helping David, a shepherd, to
become a king. Amen.

Elisha, a messenger for God

Elisha was a farmer. One day, God called him to be a special messenger.

What do you think a special messenger's job is?

THANK YOU, GOD, that You helped Elisha to be a messenger. Amen.

Sometime later, a woman called out
to Elisha for help. She didn't
have any money.

How much pocket money do you get?
How do you spend it?

THANK YOU, GOD, that Elisha knew how to
help the woman. Amen.

In her house, the woman had no
food . . . just a small jar of oil.

How would you feel if you didn't have anything to eat?

PLEASE, GOD, help those who need food. Amen.

God showed Elisha how to help.
He asked the woman to collect lots of
empty jars.

Has God ever showed you what to do? What was it?

THANK YOU, GOD, for always guiding us when we
ask for Your help. Amen.

Something special happened!
From the small jar of oil, other jars
began to fill up.

The woman was surprised and delighted!
When did you last feel like that?

THANK YOU, GOD, that You love to
give surprises. Amen.

Finally, all the jars were filled with olive oil. There wasn't one empty jar!

Do you think that this was a miracle? For another miracle from God, look at page 49.

PLEASE, GOD, let me be so happy when I see you work miracles. Amen.

The woman was so thankful. She sold all the olive oil and bought some food.

How do you show God that you are thankful?

DEAR GOD, thank You for looking after the woman with no food. Amen.

Now there was a man called Naaman.
He was very ill with a *skin* disease.

Can you pray for someone who is ill?
What is their name?

DEAR GOD, I pray for . . . Please make
them better. Amen.

A servant girl told Naaman's wife that Elisha could help Naaman.

How would you like to help someone?

THANK YOU, GOD, for using us to help others. Amen.

God showed Elisha what was best for Naaman.

God wants the best for you. Do you know why?

DEAR HEAVENLY FATHER, help me to know what is best in situations. Amen.

Through the servant girl, Elisha told
Naaman to bathe in the river.

How do you think Naaman felt when he was
told to do this?

DEAR GOD, I want to hear You when You tell
me something. Amen.

When Naaman was told to bathe in the river, he got very angry.

When was the last time you were told to
do something that you didn't want to do?

PLEASE GOD, help me to do as I am told. Amen.

Naaman didn't know God, so he
didn't understand why he should
go to the river.

Have you ever failed to do something, even though you
knew it was the right thing to do?

DEAR GOD, always teach me what is right. Amen.

Naaman's servants encouraged
Naaman, and he went to the
river to bathe.

Whom would you like to encourage today?

DEAR GOD, show me how to encourage
friends today. Amen.

When Naaman left the river . . . he was healed! Then he *believed* in God.

Do you know anyone who doesn't believe in God? What should you say to them?

PLEASE, GOD, teach me to speak to people who don't know You. Amen.

Esther . . . who helped her people

The king of Persia wanted a new wife.
So he started to search for one.

What kind of wife do you think he should
be looking for?

THANK YOU, GOD, that You found the right
wife for the king. Amen.

In Persia there lived a beautiful woman
named Esther. Her people were the
Israelites.

Who do you think is beautiful and why?

THANK YOU, GOD, for choosing Esther. Amen.

Esther loved God, but she had to keep
it a secret in the land of Persia.

Do you like talking about God?

THANK YOU, GOD, that I can talk to
people about You. Amen.

The king fell in love with Esther and they got married.
Esther became a queen.

What do you like about this story?

DEAR GOD, thank You that You chose Esther for the king to marry. Amen.

The president of Persia was called
Haman. He wanted people to bow down
and worship him.

Whom do you think we should praise and
worship?

THANK YOU, GOD, that we can come to You and praise
and worship You. Amen.

Esther and her uncle Mordecai only wanted to worship God . . . not Haman.

What other things do people worship instead
of God?

DEAR GOD, I'm so glad that I can worship
You today. Amen.

Haman didn't like Mordecai to disobey him and he got very angry.

How do you think Mordecai felt?

THANK YOU, GOD, for protecting Your people. Amen.

Wicked Haman plotted to kill Mordecai and his people, the Israelites.

Do you think Mordecai was brave because he knew that God was on his side?

YOU FIGHT FOR us. Thank You, heavenly Father. Amen.

Mordecai sent a message to Esther.
Somehow, he wanted his people
rescued.

How do you think God wanted to encourage them?

THANK YOU, GOD, that You always want to
encourage me. Amen.

Esther had a plan and she invited the king and Haman to a big banquet.

When were you last invited to a party?
What happened at the party?

DEAR GOD, thank You for inviting us to
be with You every day. Amen.

During the banquet, Esther told the king about Haman's plot. The king was shocked!

Have you ever heard bad news? What was it about?

THANK YOU, GOD, for giving Esther wisdom. Amen.

Then the king went to Haman, who
was shaking with fear. He had been
found out.

Can you sing a song about God looking after you?

DEAR GOD, help me always to follow You and
be good. Amen.

The king then stopped Haman's wicked plot and got rid of him forever.

Don't you think God is great to protect Esther, Mordecai, and all the Israelites?

I JUST WANT to sing Your praises, God, for winning this battle. Amen.

Esther and Mordecai were so pleased to hear the news that Haman had been punished.

Tell about some good news you have heard recently.

THANK YOU, GOD, for being on our side. Amen.

And so, every year Esther's people had a party because they were saved from Haman.

When will your next party be?

THANK YOU, GOD, for saving all of Esther's people. Amen.

Daniel and
the Kings

Daniel and his friends were captured
and taken to the land of Babylon.

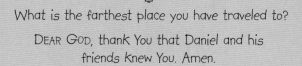

What is the farthest place you have traveled to?

DEAR GOD, thank You that Daniel and his
friends knew You. Amen.

Now Daniel and his friends were very
clever. They learned a new
foreign language.

Do you know someone who speaks a foreign language?

DEAR GOD, even though we speak different languages,
You still love us. Amen.

All four of them refused rich food and ate only vegetables. They grew strong.

Which vegetables do you enjoy eating?

THANK YOU, GOD, for being with Daniel and his friends. Amen.

One day, the king of Babylon had a dream. He asked Daniel what it meant.

Which other king had dreams? Look at page 76.

THANK YOU, GOD, for Daniel and his wisdom. Amen.

God showed Daniel the meaning of the dream. So he went to the king.

Tell something you like about Daniel.

DEAR GOD, thank You, for showing the meaning of the dream to Daniel. Amen.

Daniel explained to the king that the
dream was about a big, gold statue.

Who made Daniel wise so that he could go
to the king?

PLEASE GOD, always help me to explain wisely
to people. Amen.

The King was very pleased with Daniel and gave him many presents.

Do you like buying and giving presents?

DEAR GOD, I know You like a cheerful giver. Amen.

Then, a little later, the King built a
big gold statue.
All the people worshiped it.

What do you think is wrong with worshiping a
gold statue?

PLEASE GOD, help me to worship and look to
You, always. Amen.

Daniel's three friends refused to worship the gold statue and turned away.

Why do you think they thought it wrong to worship the statue?

DEAR GOD, You are the one holy God and I praise You. Amen.

The three friends knew it was only
right to worship their God.

Aren't you glad that you know who God is?

YOU ARE SUCH A GREAT BIG GOD. Thank You for
being my Father. Amen.

The next king of Babylon was so
pleased with Daniel that he gave him a
good job.

What job would you like to have when you grow up?

THANK YOU, GOD, that You already have a
plan for my life. Amen.

Lots of people were jealous of Daniel
and his position in the land of Babylon.

What does it mean to be jealous?

DEAR GOD, help me not to be jealous of anyone. Amen.

The people tried to make Daniel pray to the king, instead of praying to God.

If you were Daniel, what would you have thought?

THANK YOU, GOD, that Daniel only wanted to pray to You. Amen.

Daniel didn't stop praying to God . . .
and so the king threw him among
the lions.

Now how do you think Daniel felt?

THANK YOU, GOD, for sending Your angels to
be with Daniel. Amen.

The lions didn't hurt Daniel at all. The king knew that God had saved him.

What do you like about this story?

DEAR GOD, You are so mighty and save people ... especially Daniel. Amen.

Jonah and the mighty whale

God told Jonah to go to Nineveh and tell the people to behave well.

Do you think that you behave badly sometimes?

PLEASE GOD, help me not to say or do wrong things today. Amen.

But Jonah didn't want to go. He didn't like the people in Nineveh.

Are there things you don't like doing? Why?

DEAR FATHER GOD, help everybody to do what You want them to do. Amen.

So Jonah went in the opposite direction
and tried to run away from God.

Have you ever done the opposite of what you have
been told to do? What happened?

DEAR GOD, if I have done this, I'm sorry for . . .
Forgive me. Amen.

Jonah found a boat and went aboard
with other people. But God sent a
storm.

Have you ever seen a storm on the sea or a lake?

THANK YOU, GOD, that You wanted Jonah to do a
very important job. Amen.

The boat tossed and turned on the sea.
Everyone was very frightened.

Who else was caught in a storm? Look at page 29.

DEAR GOD, thank You that Jonah was still
kept safe. Amen.

Poor Jonah. He told the people in the boat that it was his fault there was a storm.

If you do something wrong, can you tell anyone about it?

FATHER GOD, help me to know if I have done wrong and to say I am sorry. Amen.

So the other men in the boat threw
Jonah overboard into the stormy sea.

If Jonah had done what God had asked, would he be
in this mess?

PLEASE GOD, help us to listen, and act upon what
You tell us to do. Amen.

At once the storm stopped and it became calm.

Can you swim? What do you like about it?

THANK YOU, GOD, even when things get difficult for us. You know all about it. Amen.

As Jonah swam, a big and mighty whale came along and swallowed him!

How do you think Jonah felt about that?

DEAR GOD, strange things sometimes happen in our lives. Help us to trust You. Amen.

For three days and nights, Jonah sat inside the whale's tummy.

Can you imagine what it was like inside of the whale?

DEAR GOD, You always have patience with us and wait. Amen.

Poor Jonah! He was in the dark and
was wet and cold. He prayed to
God for help.

Have you ever prayed to God for help?
What happened?

WHEN THINGS AREN'T going right, dear God, please
help me. Amen.

All of a sudden, the whale spat Jonah
out and he landed on the beach.

Do you think that Jonah was pleased? Do you think
God heard his prayer?

THANK YOU, GOD, for being so loving and
patient with Jonah. Amen.

Again, God told Jonah to go to Nineveh and speak to the bad people.

Do you think that Jonah will listen this time?

DEAR GOD, thank You for sometimes giving us a second chance. Amen.

This time, Jonah did as God told him to do ... and he went to Nineveh!

Is God speaking to anyone you know? Pray for them.

THANK YOU, GOD, that you can turn bad times into good times. Amen.

Jonah arrived in Nineveh. He spoke to
the bad people and they became good.

If someone were behaving badly, would you speak to
him about it?

DEAR HEAVENLY FATHER, help me to have courage
sometimes. Amen.

A special baby called Jesus is born

Mary was going to marry Joseph, when an angel came with a special message.

Do you know anyone who is getting ready for a wedding?

DEAR GOD, please take care of people who are getting married. Amen.

The angel was called Gabriel.
He told Mary that God would give
her a special baby.

Do you know anyone who is going to have a baby?

PLEASE GOD, take care of all the babies who are
going to be born. Amen.

A little later, Mary and Joseph went to Bethlehem and stayed in a stable.

What do you think it was like to stay in a stable?

DEAR HEAVENLY FATHER, thank You for finding Mary and Joseph a safe place to stay. Amen.

During the night, a baby was born and they called Him Jesus.

Sing one of your favorite Christmas carols.

THANK YOU, GOD, for giving us Your Son, Jesus. Amen.

Some shepherds came to take a look at Jesus. They praised God for Him.

What do you think the shepherds thought?

DEAR GOD, I just want to sing and praise You for sending Jesus. Amen.

Far away, some very wise men saw a star. They knew a king had been born.

The wise men had to make a long journey. Do you like long journeys?

I JUST WANT to praise You, God, for wise men. Amen.

The wise men brought gifts for Jesus
and bowed down to worship Him.

What gifts would you give your friends?

THANK YOU, GOD, for the presents the wise men
gave to Jesus. Amen.

When Jesus was a young boy, He
enjoyed playing with His friends.

What do you enjoy playing with your friends?

DEAR GOD, I want to thank You for my friends. Amen.

One day, Mary and Joseph
found Him teaching in the temple.
He was only twelve.

What do you like learning about?

THANK YOU, GOD, for giving so much
wisdom to Jesus. Amen.

As Jesus grew up, He helped Joseph,
His dad, in the carpentry shop.

Which tools does a carpenter use?

THANK YOU, GOD, that You gave such a wonderful
job to Jesus. Amen.

Jesus knew that God, His heavenly
Father, had a very special job for Him.

What are your favorite jobs at home or school?

THANK YOU, GOD, that You had already planned this
special job for Jesus. Amen.

Now Jesus' cousin, John, was
dipping people in the river and giving
them new life.

Do you know what this is called?

THANK YOU, GOD, that John baptized people. Amen.

Jesus asked John to baptize Him. Now
He was ready for that special job.

Who knows about this special job for Jesus?
Look at page 208.

YOU KNEW all along what Jesus had to do. Thank You,
God. Amen.

First, Jesus gathered together twelve
friends. They were called disciples.

Who are your best friends and what are their names?

DEAR JESUS, thank You for sending friends to me. Amen.

Jesus taught His disciples how to pray.
They followed Him everywhere.

Read today's verses, and see the prayer Jesus taught
His disciples.

DEAR LORD JESUS, I want to pray to
You every day. Amen.

Jesus,
the teacher

Jesus began to teach on a mountain.
A big crowd gathered to listen to Him.

Have you ever climbed up a very, very steep hill?

THANK YOU, JESUS, that people came to
listen to You. Amen.

He taught them that God would bless
people who looked for peace.

Where do you go when you want to be quiet?

LORD JESUS, please guide those people who are
looking for peace. Amen.

Jesus said that they should love one
another always.

What is the very best thing about having a friend?

HELP ME, LORD JESUS, to love those around me. Amen.

Jesus also taught them that they
should shine like a light in the world.

In what way do you think you could shine?

DEAR JESUS, help me to shine like a light for You. Amen.

Jesus told the crowd that they should
never boast when they talked.

What does the word "boast" mean? Have you heard
someone boast?

LORD JESUS, help me to be thoughtful when
I talk. Amen.

"Never worry," Jesus said, because He will always look after His people.

In what ways does Jesus look after you?

DEAR GOD, thank You for sending Jesus to show us what You are like. Amen.

Jesus also wanted the little ones to learn and listen to their parents.

Do you find it easy or hard to do something when you are asked?

DEAR JESUS, thank You for loving my mom and dad. Amen.

"Sometime," Jesus said, "pray quietly
when there is no one about."

Where do you like to pray and talk to Jesus?

DEAR JESUS, thank You that You like to teach us
how to pray. Amen.

Jesus said, "Never point a finger at a person when they do wrong."

Has anyone pointed a finger at you?
What did they say?

DEAR JESUS, help me not to say wrong things about people. Amen.

Jesus also taught the crowd to search for Him and God, his heavenly Father.

If you had to look for God today, where would you look?

THANK YOU, GOD, for the sky, sea, mountains, little animals, and Your word in the Bible. Amen.

Jesus told the crowd that there were
great riches in heaven.

What do you treasure the most?

THANK YOU, JESUS, that You are so, so special. Amen.

They were to ask God for all that they needed, and God would take care of them.

What would you like to ask God to provide for you, or someone you know, today?

THANK YOU, GOD, for my food, clothes, and my family. Amen.

Jesus taught people to be very careful whom they listened to.

Where can we learn more about what Jesus said?

OUR FATHER, who is in heaven, holy is Your name. Amen.

Jesus said that they were to be wise
and listen to Him to avoid trouble.

Which stories in the Bible do you enjoy listening to?

LORD JESUS, help me and teach me to be wise. Amen.

When Jesus finished speaking, the crowd was amazed at His teaching!

What did you think about Jesus' teaching?

DEAR JESUS, because You teach me what is good, I want to follow You every day. Amen.

Jesus helps a
little girl

A man named Jairus went to Jesus. His daughter was very ill, nearly dying.

Do you know someone who is not well?

DEAR LORD JESUS, please help . . . to feel better today. Amen.

"Please, please come and see my daughter. I want her well," said Jairus.

How can I help a person who is not feeling well?

WHEN A PERSON is ill, please Jesus, teach me to show how much I care. Amen.

So Jesus made His way to the home of Jairus.

What do you like about Jesus when you talk to Him?

DEAR JESUS, thank You for always going where You are needed. Amen.

On the way, a person ran up to them
and said, "Jairus' daughter is dead."

How do you think Jairus must have felt?

LORD JESUS, please help people who have had news that
someone they love has died. Amen.

The man told Jairus not to bother
Jesus anymore. He thought that Jesus
was too busy.

Do you think this was a wrong or right thing to say?

THANK YOU, JESUS, that You are never too busy to
help us. Amen.

Jesus lovingly told Jairus not to be
afraid. He was just to have faith in Him.

Is there something you are worried about at
the moment?

LORD JESUS, when I am worried, You help me.
Thank You. Amen.

When Jesus arrived at the house, there was a big crowd. They all were crying.

Can you talk about a time when you have been upset?

DEAR JESUS, thank You that I can come to You when I am upset. Amen.

Jesus went into the house. He took
three disciples, also Jairus and his wife.

Think of a time when you asked for help and
Jesus answered.

THANK YOU, JESUS, that You wanted to help
Jairus' family. Amen.

The crowd was still crying. So Jesus told them to stop.

When have you cried? What did you cry about?

DEAR JESUS, when I cry, thank You for being there too. Amen.

Jesus told the crowd that the little girl
was not dead ... only sleeping.

What things do you like about Jesus in this story?

THANK YOU, JESUS, that sometimes You like to
surprise us. Amen.

The crowd didn't believe what Jesus had said . . . and they laughed at Him.

Do you know someone who doesn't believe in Jesus?

DEAR JESUS, thank You that You came into the world to help people. Amen.

Jesus went to the little girl and gently said that she was to get up.

Do you think that Jesus is very gentle?

THANK YOU, DEAR JESUS, for being so gentle. Amen.

The little girl opened her eyes and then stood up!

Doesn't this story make you want to praise and thank Jesus?

LORD JESUS, You knew all along how to help this little girl. Thank You. Amen.

When Jairus and his wife saw what had happened, they were amazed.

Have you ever been amazed about something?

JESUS, You know how to make me happy. Thank You for being so special. Amen.

Mom and Dad were so happy.
They hugged their daughter and gave
her a meal.

What do you like about being hugged?

THANK YOU, JESUS, that You made the little
girl better. Amen

Jesus and a miracle

Jesus wanted to spend time with His disciples. So they went to Bethsaida.

Who do you like to spend time with, and why?

THANK YOU, JESUS, for encouraging us to have quiet times with our friends. Amen.

People followed Jesus to Bethsaida.
They heard that He had done
great things.

What great things have you heard about Jesus?

DEAR JESUS, thank You for Your great patience and
love toward us. Amen.

Jesus welcomed the crowd and spoke to
them about God, His heavenly Father.

Do you know people who talk about God and Jesus?
What are their names?

DEAR JESUS, help me to speak about
You and God. Amen.

Jesus also healed many people in the
crowd because He loved them.

When a person is ill, can you think of a special gift to
take to them?

THANK YOU, JESUS, You know what's best for
people. Amen.

In the evening, the disciples told Jesus
to send the crowd home to eat.

What do you like best when you go home?

DEAR LORD JESUS, thank You for my home. Amen.

But Jesus didn't want them to go home because He wanted to feed them.

The crowd had listened to Jesus all day. Do you think they were hungry?

THANK YOU, JESUS, for giving us food when we are hungry. Amen.

The disciples were astonished because there were 5,000 people. That's a lot!

Can you remember a party you've been to?
How many people came?

DEAR JESUS, for You it was not a problem to feed ALL
of those people. Thank You. Amen.

They didn't know where they could find enough food for all the people.

In poor countries, people have to search for food. How can we help them?

THANK YOU, JESUS, for helping me to help poor people. Amen.

At last, Andrew, one of the disciples, found a little boy with some food.

Do you know anyone who shares food with you? Do you share your food?

DEAR JESUS, thank You for this little boy who wanted to give his food. Amen.

But it wasn't very much at all . . . only
five loaves and two small fish!

What would you feed a friend if he were hungry?

WHEN A PERSON has very little, help me to be kind and
thoughtful to him. Amen.

The disciples told Jesus that this food would not feed 5,000 people.

Do you trust Jesus? Are you sure of what He is doing?

THANK YOU, JESUS, that we can trust You to feed 5,000 people. Amen.

However, Jesus asked the crowd to sit
down on the grass.

Have you ever been on a picnic? Where did you go?

DEAR JESUS, thank You that it is so enjoyable to
eat outside. Amen.

Then Jesus took the two small fish and five loaves and said grace.

Do you say grace before a meal?

THANK YOU, LORD JESUS, that You can do great things with small offerings we give. Amen.

The small fish and loaves fed ALL of the crowd, and they were full.

What do you enjoy eating when you go on a picnic?

DEAR JESUS, thank You that we can feel full after a meal. Amen.

Feeding the crowd was a miracle, and the crowd was amazed!

When have you been amazed the most?

THANK YOU, JESUS, for all Your miracles. Amen

A man who cared

One day a very important man asked Jesus a question.

What questions would you like to ask Jesus?

DEAR JESUS, thank You that we can come to you because you have the answers. Amen.

The very important man wanted to know about loving his neighbor.

Who are your neighbors?

DEAR LORD JESUS, thank You for the people next door. Amen.

Then Jesus told a story to
the very important man about
helping other people.

Do you know anyone who helps other people?

DEAR JESUS, please show me who needs
help in the world. Amen.

Jesus said, "A man was traveling from
Jerusalem to Jericho . . . "

Try to find Jerusalem in an atlas.

JESUS, thank You for teaching us through
Your stories. Amen.

Suddenly, two robbers pounced on the traveller and beat him up.

Have you ever seen anyone being bullied at your school?

PLEASE JESUS, protect me and my friends at school. Amen.

The poor traveller was very injured. He was nearly dying.

What do you think is bad about robbers?

THANK YOU, JESUS that not only do you watch over us but over robbers as well. Amen.

A little later on, a priest walked
down the road. But he didn't stop to
help the traveler.

What would you have done if you had been
walking down the road?

PLEASE, JESUS, help me to stop what I am doing and
help other people. Amen.

Then, a man who worked in the
Jerusalem temple walked by.
He didn't stop either.

What are your thoughts on these two men who walked
past the traveler?

DEAR LORD JESUS, I know You would have stopped to
help. Thank You. Amen.

Another man came by who was an
enemy of the traveler.
He saw him and stopped.

Do you know of any people who help the
suffering in the world?

THANK YOU, JESUS, for the love of this man, even though
he was an enemy. Amen.

The enemy knelt down and gently cleaned and bandaged the traveler's wounds.

When you fall over, who helps to pick you up?

THANK YOU, JESUS, when I fall down, You are always there to help me. Amen.

The enemy put the traveler on
his donkey and took him to
the nearest hotel.

Have you ever stayed in a hotel? Do you know
a friend who has?

DEAR JESUS, thank You that You knew what the
traveler needed. Amen.

Then the enemy asked the innkeeper to take care of the injured traveler.

Even though this man was an enemy, what was good about him?

PLEASE, JESUS, help me to help people, even if they don't like me. Amen.

The enemy kindly told the innkeeper
that he would pay for the
traveler's stay.

Can you think of four good things about the enemy?

THANK YOU, LORD JESUS, that You can give us love for
people we don't like. Amen.

Jesus then asked the very important
man who the most loving person was.

Which one do you think was the most loving and caring
person in this story?

DEAR JESUS, help me to remember to say "thank you"
when someone helps me. Amen.

Then Jesus told the very important man
to be like the person who loved to help.

How can you comfort someone who has fallen
down and hurt himself?

WHEN SOMEONE NEEDS help, dear Jesus, may I be the
one to go and comfort him. Amen.

Something lost and found

Jesus wanted people to know that He
cared for the lonely and lost.

Do you know any lonely people?

DEAR JESUS, show me how I can help people
who live alone. Amen.

So Jesus told them a story . . . "A
shepherd had one hundred sheep . . . "

What do you like when you see sheep in
the countryside?

THANK YOU, HEAVENLY FATHER, for making the
countryside and sheep. Amen.

One day the shepherd noticed that
there was one sheep missing.
It was lost.

Have you ever lost anything? How did you feel?

DEAR JESUS, when I lose something, help me to
find it. Thank You. Amen.

So the shepherd left the
other ninety-nine to go looking for
the lost sheep.

Who else looked after sheep? Look at page 118.

THANK YOU, JESUS, for shepherds and
farmers everywhere. Amen.

The shepherd searched and searched
everywhere for the missing sheep.

When you *lose* something, who helps you to find it?

DEAR JESUS, when I *lose* something, it makes me sad.
Help me to be happy. Amen.

The poor sheep was lost and all alone. Perhaps it was frightened.

How do you think Jesus felt about this lost sheep?

THANK YOU, JESUS, that You don't want any one of us lost. Amen.

At last the shepherd found the sheep!
He was so happy.

How do you feel when you find something that
you have lost?

THANK YOU, JESUS, You are with us when we lose
something. You comfort us. Amen.

Jesus told another story about
things lost and found, to teach us
of God's love.

What did you like about the last story?

JESUS, thank You that your care and love is
SO, SO big. Amen.

Jesus said, "There was a woman who lost a coin from her headdress."

If you lost some of your money, how would you feel?

DEAR LORD JESUS, help me not to lose my money. Amen.

So she lit a lamp and searched and searched for the coin in her home.

In Jesus' time, how was the lighting different from today?

THANK YOU, JESUS, that the woman didn't give up searching. Amen.

Finally, after much searching, the
woman found her lost coin.

If you found some money, what would you do with it?

DEAR JESUS, help me to know that everything
belongs to God. Amen.

The woman was so happy that she ran
out of the house to tell her friends.

How do you think her friends felt? How do you feel
when you find something?

THANK YOU, LORD JESUS, that when I am happy,
my friends are happy too. Amen.

"God is like this too," Jesus told the
crowd. He is happy when He finds us.

Are you happy God has found you? What makes you
happy about knowing God?

THANK YOU, GOD, that you found me and that You want
to be a friend to me. Amen.

A son who ran away

Jesus told another story about a
farmer with two sons.

Have you ever visited a farm? What did you
like about it?

DEAR GOD, thank You for farms everywhere.
Please take care of them. Amen.

One day, the younger son asked
his father for his share of
money from the farm.

This younger son thought that he would be better by
himself. Is this right or wrong?

DEAR JESUS, thank You for my home and
my family. Amen.

This made the father sad, but he gave his son the money and waved goodbye.

When you say goodbye to someone, how do you feel?

DEAR HEAVENLY FATHER, please be with me when I start a journey. Amen.

The youngest son wanted to live life to the full . . . with lots of excitement.

What do you like best . . . looking forward to a party or the party itself?

DEAR JESUS, help me to be happy day by day and enjoy being with You. Amen.

He traveled to a faraway country and spent his money on all sorts of things.

Tell how you have spent your money on something good . . . and on something bad.

HELP ME, LORD JESUS, to spend my money wisely and to take care of it. Amen.

Soon he ran out of money. He had no food and his friends left him.

Do you think they were true friends?

DEAR LORD JESUS, be with me and my friends, whom I love. Amen.

So, the youngest son had to get a job.
It wasn't a very clean one . . .
feeding pigs.

Do you have a pet animal? Do you enjoy feeding it?

DEAR JESUS, you still loved this son, even though
he went his own way. Amen.

No one gave him anything to eat.
He was so unhappy.

Do you feel sorry for this youngest son and
what he did?

THANK YOU, LORD JESUS, that You don't want us
to be unhappy. Amen.

The youngest son began to think that he had been very silly.

Have you ever done a silly thing and wished you hadn't?

DEAR JESUS, help me to think in a wise way.
Thank you. Amen.

So he thought it would be
better to return home and say
"sorry" to his father.

Is there anyone you should say "sorry" to?

WHEN I DO wrong, help me to say
"sorry," Jesus. Amen.

The father spotted his youngest son coming towards the farm.

Do you think that the father was glad to
see his son? Why?

THANK YOU, GOD, that you will never leave me. Amen.

He ran toward his youngest son and
gave him a big hug. He was so pleased.

Who do you love to hug?

DEAR JESUS, thank You that the father forgave
his son. Amen.

Then he immediately gave a big party
with music for his youngest son.

What sort of music do you like and why?

THERE ARE SO many ways that You show Your love, Jesus.
Thank You. Amen.

But the older son felt left out. He had never run away like his brother.

Do you ever feel left out of things? When did this happen?

THANK YOU, JESUS, that You always know how we feel. Amen.

Then the father said, although one
son was lost and found again, he
loved them both.

In your family, how do you like to celebrate a
special event?

THANK YOU, LORD JESUS, that You love us
all the same. Amen.

Jesus and the little ones

Jesus loved to be with the little ones.
And they enjoyed being with him.

Where are you going tomorrow?
Do you think that Jesus would like to go with you?

THANK YOU, JESUS. Where You go, I want to go. Amen.

One day, the disciples came to
Jesus and asked who was the greatest
in the kingdom.

What does "the kingdom" mean to you?
Who belongs to it?

DEAR LORD JESUS, I want to be in Your kingdom. Amen.

Then Jesus called to a little one and stood him in the middle of them all.

What are the good things about being small?

LORD JESUS, it doesn't matter to You whether we are too small. You still love us. Amen.

Jesus explained to his disciples that
their hearts should become
like a child's.

How do you think the disciples felt when
Jesus said this?

DEAR JESUS, thank You for loving every child in
the world. Amen.

He said to them that they must be humble. Then they would be the greatest in the kingdom.

What do you think the word "humble" means?

THANK YOU, JESUS, that we can become like You. Amen.

Jesus said to His disciples that whoever welcomes little ones . . . welcomes Him.

Who do you like to welcome into your home?

JESUS, thank You for always welcoming me with open arms. Amen.

Then lots of grown-ups brought the little children to Jesus.

Do you go to Sunday school?
What do you enjoy about it?

THANK YOU, JESUS, that I am very important to You. Amen.

They wanted Jesus to bless and pray for the little ones.

Does your family pray for a blessing for you?

DEAR LORD JESUS, I pray for a blessing on my family and my friends. Amen.

But the disciples were upset because
the children were brought to Jesus.

What do you think about the disciples being upset?

THANK YOU, JESUS, that You were glad the
children came to you. Amen.

Jesus corrected the disciples. He said they were not to stop the children from coming to Him.

What stories do you like to hear about Jesus?

HEAVENLY FATHER GOD, I want to praise Your name for Jesus. Amen.

"These are My little ones," Jesus said,
"and they belong to Me."

What other ways does Jesus make you feel special?

DEAR JESUS, I just want everyone to know how
great You are. Amen.

Then Jesus placed His hands on the
little ones' heads and blessed them.

Does this make you want to love
Jesus more and more?

DEAR JESUS, I just want to say how much I
love You. Amen.

Jesus also wanted the little ones to learn and listen to their parents.

✤

Do you find it easy or hard to do something when you are asked?

DEAR JESUS, thank You for loving my mom and dad. Amen.

Jesus said that all children were to be treated kindly, for angels take care of them.

Can you remember the name of the angel who visited Mary? Look at page 197.

THANK YOU, LORD JESUS, for sending angels to take care of me. Amen.

Jesus so loved the little ones because they sang praises to Him.

Do you enjoy singing? What is your favorite song about Jesus?

DEAR LORD JESUS, I want to wake up in the morning singing praises to You. Amen.

A small man with a lot of money

Meet Zacchaeus. He lived in Jericho.
He was a very small man.

Tell about some good things that happen to you when you are small.

LORD JESUS, thank You for knowing Zacchaeus, just like You know me. Amen.

Zacchaeus was a very important tax collector. He had a lot of money.

Do you know of any important people you can pray for?

DEAR GOD, please guide and care for . . . Thank You. Amen.

One day, Jesus went to Jericho and He walked through the town.

What is the name of your town or village?

I PRAY FOR every person who lives in my city/town/village. Amen.

Zacchaeus ran as fast as he could.
He was excited because he
wanted to see Jesus. . .

When do you get excited about seeing someone?

DEAR JESUS, let me be excited about
You every day. Amen.

. . . but he couldn't. Zacchaeus was far
too small and the crowd was far too big!

What do you like about being in a crowd?
What don't you like?

THANK YOU, JESUS, for Zacchaeus, who just
wanted to see You. Amen.

So Zacchaeus climbed a tree so that
he could see Jesus much better.

What are some good things about trees?

DEAR JESUS, thank You that Zacchaeus was so
excited to see You. Amen.

When Jesus reached the tree, He looked up and saw Zacchaeus.

How do you think Zacchaeus felt when Jesus looked at him?

DEAR JESUS, You knew all about Zacchaeus and you loved Him. Amen.

"Come down," Jesus said to Zacchaeus.
"I want to visit your home."

If you had an invitation from Jesus, what would be the
first thing you would do?

THANK YOU, JESUS, that You wanted to change
Zacchaeus' heart. Amen.

Zaccheus came down from
the tree. He felt *so* proud that Jesus
had called him.

If Jesus called you today, would you like to
follow Him? Why?

I AM SO glad that You call each one of us,
dear Jesus. Amen.

The crowd didn't like Zacchaeus meeting Jesus. They thought Zacchaeus was a cheat.

What do you think? Was it right for Jesus to talk to Zacchaeus? Look at the prayer on page 326.

THANK YOU, JESUS, that You are willing to talk to all types of people. Amen.

Zacchaeus was very happy because he was a friend of Jesus.

What makes you happy about being a friend of Jesus?

THANK YOU, JESUS, that I can call You my Friend. Amen.

Zacchaeus was *so* delighted to
walk with Jesus that he wanted to
give something.

What would you like to give to Jesus?

DEAR JESUS, I give You my heart today. Amen.

"I'll give half of my money to the poor,"
Zacchaeus said to Jesus.

How can giving your money to the poor help them?

DEAR LORD JESUS, teach me to give some of
my money away. Amen.

" . . . and if I have cheated anyone with money, I'll pay them back more!"

Do you think Jesus was pleased with Zacchaeus? Why?

THANK YOU, DEAR JESUS, for touching Zacchaeus' heart. Amen.

Jesus forgave Zacchaeus for being a cheat. Zacchaeus was SO happy.

What do you like about this story?

THANK YOU, JESUS, that You forgave and loved Zacchaeus. Amen.

An invite to a wonderful party

Jesus loved to tell stories of His kingdom. They are called parables.

Can you think of another parable you have read?

THANK YOU, JESUS, because You love to teach me. Amen.

One of Jesus' parables is about a rich
man who wanted to give a party.

What special occasions would you give a party for?

DEAR LORD JESUS, I love to hear about
Your parables. Amen.

The rich man made a list of all the
people he wanted to invite to his party.

Do you know anyone who makes lists for anything?
What are they for?

THANK YOU, JESUS, for all the good parties
I go to. Amen

The servants of the rich man worked very hard getting all the food ready.

What is your favorite food at a party?

DEAR JESUS, thank You for providing our food on special occasions. Amen.

The table looked splendid for
the party with lots of
food, decorations, and flowers.

During the year, when do we decorate a table to
look special?

DEAR JESUS, help me to lay the table to
look pretty. Amen.

Then the rich man sent out a
servant to call all the invited guests to
the party.

How many friends did you have at your last party?

THANK YOU, JESUS, that You call us by name. Amen.

But there was a big surprise for
the servant when he called on
the first guest.

Have you invited a friend for a meal and they
have said "No"?

DEAR JESUS, let me always go on loving my friends,
whatever happens. Amen.

"Sorry," he said, "I've got to go to my fields. I can't come to the party."

If you knew God wanted you to do something, what would you say?

THANK YOU, JESUS, that You encourage me to do the right thing. Amen.

The servant went to the second guest.
"The party is ready," he said.

Do you get excited when you are going to parties?

DEAR JESUS, thank You for parties that I
can enjoy. Amen.

"Sorry," said the second guest.
"I'm going to see some of my animals.
I can't come."

Have you ever heard anyone make excuses?

DEAR LORD JESUS, please help me to understand
my friends. Amen.

Each guest the servant asked said,
"No, I can't go to the party."

Have you ever felt disappointed when something
hasn't happened?

DEAR LORD JESUS, I know You are with me when I get
disappointed. Thank You. Amen.

The rich man was very angry.
He looked at all the food . . . and
had an idea.

What is the best idea you have ever had?

DEAR JESUS, I love it when You turn bad
into good. Amen.

The rich man said, "Invite all
the poor people, the blind and crippled
to the party."

Why do you think that this was a good idea?

THANK YOU, GOD, for being such a loving, caring,
thoughtful, and good God. Amen.

How great! The party was full of
people who wanted to be there.

What do you like about this parable?

PLEASE, JESUS, help me to follow You everywhere. Amen.

Jesus said that when God invites us to be with Him, we should be willing to go.

How do you join God's family? Look at the prayer at the end of this book.

DEAR JESUS, I want to hear You when You call me. Amen.

Jesus dies . . . but it's not the end!

Jesus and His disciples were traveling to Jerusalem.

What country is Jerusalem in? Look in your atlas to find it.

DEAR JESUS, thank You for your disciples who wanted to follow you. Amen.

On their way, Jesus asked two of
the disciples to fetch a donkey for
Him to ride.

Describe what a donkey looks like and what color it is.

THANK YOU, JESUS, for that very special donkey. Amen.

Jesus rode into Jerusalem on
the donkey. Lots of people cheered and
welcomed Him.

Read today's verse. How would you welcome Jesus?

DEAR LORD JESUS, I want to cheer and praise You. Amen.

Some of the crowd spread palm
branches on the road in front of Jesus.
They sang too.

What song would you sing to praise Jesus?

THANK YOU, JESUS, for the crowd who gave such a
big welcome. Amen.

Some of the leaders hated Jesus,
because they were jealous.
They planned to kill Him.

Do you know what being jealous is?

THANK YOU, JESUS, for all Your teaching and
miracles. Amen.

Jesus knew that He was going to die.
At supper, Jesus said goodbye to
His disciples.

How do you think the disciples felt about Jesus dying?

THANK YOU, JESUS, that I will never, ever have to
say goodbye to you. Amen.

Jesus tore off some bread and poured
some drink. "Take this," he said, "and
remember me."

How do you remember Jesus each day?

DEAR LORD JESUS, thank You that I am reminded of
You, when . . . Amen.

After the meal, Jesus went into a
garden and prayed to God. . .
His heavenly Father.

Read today's verses and see what Jesus prayed.

I JUST WANT to thank You, Jesus, for all that You have
done for me. Amen.

Then some soldiers came and
arrested Jesus. They took Him before
the leaders.

Can you remember some of the wonderful things
Jesus had done?

DEAR JESUS, it must have been painful for You. Thank
You for doing it for me. Amen.

The leaders, who were enemies of
Jesus, put Him on a cross. He died.

But there is a wonderful surprise. Do you think
Jesus likes to give surprises?

THANK YOU, DEAR JESUS, for dying for all the
wrong in the world. Amen.

Jesus' body was wrapped up and
put in a tomb. A stone was rolled in
front of it.

This seems like the end . . . but read today's verses.

DEAR FATHER GOD in heaven, thank You for giving us
Your Son Jesus. Amen.

Two friends of Jesus visited the
tomb shortly afterward . . . they
found it empty!

This was the surprise! What is the best surprise
you've ever had?

THANK YOU, JESUS, that You are alive today. Amen.

An angel said that the disciples were to go to Galilee to meet Jesus.

An angel is a messenger. What other angel gave a message? Look at page 197.

DEAR LORD JESUS, I'm so happy that an angel gave such good news. Thank You. Amen.

"Tell the whole world," Jesus said to them, "about Me and my heavenly Father."

Do you like talking about Jesus to friends? What do you tell them?

THANK YOU, JESUS, that there is SO much to say about You. Amen.

Then Jesus went to heaven to be with Father God. He is now alive forever!

One day You will meet Jesus. How do you feel about that?

DEAR JESUS, thank You for heaven, because You are there. Amen.

Spreading the good news

Before the disciples talked about Jesus,
they needed some special help.

In your neighborhood, do you know anyone who
needs help?

DEAR GOD, thank You that You are such a big and
powerful God. Amen.

The disciples went to an upstairs room
to wait for this special help.

When have you had to wait for something?

THANK YOU, JESUS, that while I wait, You are
with me. Amen.

Suddenly, in the room, there was a
sound like a roaring and rushing wind.

What do You like about really windy days?

THANK YOU, LORD JESUS, for the Holy Spirit, that blows
like the wind.

God's help had come . . .
the Holy Spirit!
All of the disciples were filled with joy.

Read today's verses on what the Holy Spirit did.

DEAR GOD, thank You for giving the disciples Your
Holy Spirit. Amen.

Now the disciples knew that they could
speak boldly about God and Jesus.

Why is Jesus special to you?

LORD JESUS, with the help of the Holy Spirit, let me
be bold for You. Amen.

The disciples amazed everyone by telling all the people about God's love.

This was the birthday of the Church. When is your birthday?

DEAR JESUS, I pray for everyone who has a birthday today. Amen.

The crowd wanted to learn about Jesus. Peter, one of the disciples, spoke to them.

What do you enjoy learning about Jesus?

DEAR GOD, with the help of the Holy Spirit, show me more about Jesus. Amen.

He told the crowd about Jesus'
miracles and Jesus dying and
coming to life again.

Tell someone about one of Jesus' miracles.

JESUS, You did so much for all of us in the world.
Thank You. Amen.

"Turn away from bad and say you are sorry to Jesus," Peter told them.

When you do something wrong, do you say "sorry" to Jesus?

LORD JESUS, I am so sorry when I've done something wrong. Amen.

Peter also told them to call out to
Jesus because He would help them.

Have you ever called out to Jesus?

DEAR LORD JESUS, when I call for help, will you please
be with me? Amen.

Another man who loved to tell people about Jesus was Paul.

What is good about telling friends about Jesus?

DEAR JESUS, thank You for Paul, who loved You . . . like me! Amen.

Paul had many adventures going to tell people about Jesus.

What exciting day do you look forward to?

THANK YOU, JESUS, that it's a very exciting adventure following You. Amen.

Paul traveled to many countries. He told everyone he met about Jesus.

What are people called who travel to other countries to talk about Jesus?

THANK YOU, HEAVENLY FATHER, for missionaries. Please keep them safe. Amen.

Paul wrote many letters about the love,
forgiveness and peace of God.

Do you ever write letters or notes to anyone? Who?

THANK YOU, DEAR JESUS, for all we learn about You from
Paul. Amen.

Paul also said that the Lord Jesus has promised to return again!

When Jesus returns, what do you think He will change?

DEAR JESUS, I love You and look forward to You coming back. Amen.